D1197525

Chicken Train
Poems from the Arkansas Delta

by Terry Minchow-Proffitt

Chicken Train: Poems from the Arkansas Delta
Copyright © 2016 by Terry Minchow-Proffitt
All rights reserved.

Grateful acknowledgement to the editors of these journals where the following poems originally appeared, or are forthcoming, at times in slightly altered forms:

"An Early Exit" *Wild Violet Literary Magazine*
"Chicken Train" *Broad Street Magazine*
"Bad Memory" *Black Fox Literary Magazine*
"Bivouac" *Big Muddy: A Journal of the Mississippi River Valley*
"Bonanza" *Organs of Vision and Speech Magazine*
"Doing My Best Father" *Eunoia Review*
"Gasoline" *Valparaiso Poetry Review* & *Wild Violet Literary Magazine*
"Hamartia" *Freshwater Review*
"Later," "Midway," "Helena Bound" *Deep South Magazine*
"Living Water" *Crux Literary Journal* & *The Examined Life Journal*
"Out Here" *Arkansas Review*
"Proceedings of . . . the Rock Solid Association" *Crack the Spine Literary Magazine*
"Rivervale, Arkansas" *Prick of the Spindle*
"Secondhand Smoke" *Oxford American*
"The Time of the Snow" *The Tower Journal*
"This Blanched Abrasion We Call *In*" *Valparaiso Poetry Review*
"What Momma John Called to Say" *Crux Literary Journal*
"Wonder Bread" *Whole Terrain*

ISBN-13: 978-0692711828
ISBN-10: 0692711821

Cover and book design by Hannah Minchow-Proffitt
Photography by Terry Minchow-Proffitt or used by permission of family members
Photo editing by Elim Allee

Published by Middle Island Press
PO Box 354
West Union, WV 26456
middleislandpress.com

A Note on the Type

This book is set in Grad (2004), which was designed by Phil Martin as a redesign of Century Schoolbook. Martin is the designer of over 400 typefaces, and created Grad for his personal use prior to bringing it to Mark Simonson who modernized it into an OpenType font.

Also by Terry Minchow-Proffitt:

Seven Last Words (2015)

For my mother, father, and sisters,
who taught me always to remember who I am.

And for my wife, Sandy, and our children, Zak and Hannah,
who hold my heart.

CONTENTS

Foreword   11

Delta, Ghosts, and Grace   13

Flat Black Fields Rimmed by a Scribble of Scrub Oak   20

PART I

Chicken Train   26

Keen Lucinda   31

On Hearing About Uncle Billy   32

Lehi   34

This Blanched Abrasion We Call *In*   36

Secondhand Alligator   38

Proceedings of the 15th Annual Session of the Rock Solid Association   41

Midway   43

Wonder Bread   45

Bivouac   48

Rex Café and Motel   51

Out Here   55

Bonanza   56

Hamartia   59

Helena Bound   60

PART II

Chickens in the Rain   67

To a Green Patch of Yard   68

Mojo   70

Sharp Relief   71

What Momma John Called to Say   73

The Front   77

Bad Memory   80

Later   82

Telling Time   83

Secondhand Smoke   86

Doing My Best Father   87

Living Water   89

The Time of the Snow   93

Rivervale, Arkansas   95

Gasoline   97

An Early Exit   100

Acknowledgments   103

About the Contributors   104

Original Dyess Home on Last Legs: Off Highway 14

FOREWORD

15 June 2016
Ozark, Missouri

Dear Terry,

When I was young and learning to play guitar, a much older musician explained to me that the best music happens within the space around the notes that are left out. By the same token, I have always agreed with the definition of poetry as the proper usage of white space on the page. But it's difficult for me to imagine finding the proper usage of white space in a book of poetry about the Arkansas Delta, the place where I grew up and came of age. There is just so much, too much really. The wells of passion, beauty, cruelty, hope, and dread are deep and rich, and the ghosts that reside there are, as you say, protective and formidable. I have often thought that some of the best writers in the world are from the South because of the vast cultural complexity of that world. The foreboding beauty of the land and its people lends itself perfectly to creative prose. But with a book of poetry about life in the Arkansas Delta, how do you choose which notes to leave out?

You nailed it, man. Captured it. Timeworn Delta memories forever trapped in amber. Your words. All of these feelings, so hard to talk about now. How did you do it? How deep did you have to go to bring all of this back to the surface?

After all of the years away, my memories of this place, this time, had become blurred and tattered like old sepia-tone pictures from a long-ago world, long since gone. Now, your words have brought them all back into view, beautiful and clear. You've made it possible to touch again those fading buildings and smell the dark gumbo dirt and heavy, languid air. I remember it all now, thanks to you. I know these people. I know their faces. I have listened to their dreams and felt their fears. I have hung on every word, and I have followed their directions. And the roads I have traveled from this place have served me well. After reading your words I understand that everything I had been seeking was just under the surface all the time, pushing me, inspiring me, frightening me, as part of that fabric of home which set the course for the journey. The Delta.

I am so grateful for your work, this work. And it is indeed an honor to be included by the use of our lyrics. Every region of the planet has its mystery, its darkness, and its light. And every place, especially a place like the Arkansas Delta, needs its voice, its champion, and its guide. Now, for me, when I think of who I am, and where I come from, that voice will be yours.

John Dillon
Ozark Mountain Daredevils

Train Track: Between Luxora and Oseola, Arkansas

DELTA, GHOSTS, AND GRACE

Fifteen apparitions have I seen;
The worst a coat upon a coat-hanger.
     –WILLIAM YEATS, "The Apparitions"

DELTA

These poems run deep with home: leaving home, returning home, grieving home. I left the Arkansas Delta, the place of my raising, when I graduated from college in 1979. Since then, two-thirds of my days have been spent beyond the Mid-South, in places out West, back East, and now, Midwest, here in St. Louis. My current home bears a striking similarity to the Delta, at least in terms of sweltering summers, an appreciation for the blues, a rabid love for the Cardinals, and the presence of the ever-mesmerizing Mississippi River. No matter where I've lived, I keep "homing back" South to the Arkansas Delta as my True North.

I've been a part of the Delta diaspora long enough to grow accustomed to confused looks over my casual references to "The Delta." Some, a very small number, think in terms of calculus and quadratic equations, others of the fourth letter of the Greek alphabet. Still others might flash on the technically true delta of the Mississippi, the southern tip where Old Man River surrenders to the Gulf of Mexico. Even those who are aware of the Mississippi Delta made famous by the likes of William Faulkner, Shelby Foote, and Eudora Welty, usually think solely in terms of the Mississippi-side. They picture that fertile alluvial plain hemmed in by the Mississippi and Yazoo rivers that stretches 200 miles long and 70 miles across at its widest point, roughly from Memphis south to Natchez.

Bless their hearts. They're close, but the Arkansas Delta is a tad farther west, just on the other side of the Mississippi River. Cross the river on I-40 West at Memphis, or, farther south, take the bridge where Highway 49 North crosses into Helena-West Helena, just a few miles from the crossroads with Highway 61, where blues legend Robert Johnson made his deal with the Devil. There you'll find the same Mississippi Alluvial Plain. With rich topsoil up to 50-plus feet deep in some places, the Arkansas Delta spreads as far west as Little Rock, and traces the Mississippi River some 250 miles south along the eastern border of the state to Louisiana. This is River Country, where coffee-colored bayous, streams, and rivers of varying sizes meander into the Mississippi: the Black, Bayou de View, St. Francis, L'Anguille, Cache, White, Big Creek, Bayou La Grue, Bayon Meto, Arkansas, Bayou Bartholomew, Bayou Macon, and Boeuf. This is a land of famously gifted native sons and daughters: writers like Douglas Blackmon, John Grisham, Jo McDougle, Lily Peter, Grif Stockley, Jr., Miller Williams, and Richard Wright; widely diverse musicians who till the rural air aural, such as Black Oak Arkansas, Ed Bruce, Johnny Cash, Iris Dement, John Dillon, Al Green, Levon Helm, Buddy Jewell, Louis Jordan, Robert Lockwood, Jr., Charlie Rich, Sister Rosetta Tharpe, Conway Twitty, William Warfield, and Sonny Boy Williamson II; progressive politicians and activists like William Alexander, Jr., and Hattie Carraway; and athletes and coaches of such accomplishment as Gene Bearden, Earl Bell, Kenny Hatfield, Robert L. Hill, Don Kessinger, Guy Kochel, Jr., Sonny Liston, Margaret Kaelin McHugh, Scottie

Pippen, and "Bones" Taylor.

I'll allow that the Delta's big and vast, but also varied—and pridefully particular. These poems stem from the Arkansas Delta. In fact, think smaller still. Get a bead on that part of eastern Arkansas that lies between Crowley's Ridge and the Mississippi River. From its best reach in the north, about 50 miles across, picture a lowland that hugs the Mississippi River in an ever-narrowing approach, as Crowley's Ridge ranges southeast for 140 miles to converge with the river at Helena-West Helena. Though never higher than 300-500 feet, these modest hills might as well be the Ozarks compared to the flat Delta plain they overlook. In fact, due to their higher elevation and the dusty but rich loess soil, much of the ridge's vegetation is of an upland variety found nowhere else in the area. Early on, settlers took to this high ground to avoid the constant threat of flooding. Accordingly, many of the oldest towns of the Arkansas Delta lie along these rolling hills: Piggott, Paragould, and Jonesboro in the north; Wynne, Forrest City, and Helena-West Helena to the south. The Delta lowlands, by contrast, are speckled with towns laid out on unstable gumbo quagmire, a dark, sticky soil that constantly contracts and expands with the weather. Though the area is now largely protected from the Mississippi's erratic ways by levees, the miry gumbo soil has a remarkable ability to retain water, so sloughs abound and floods remain a threat in cities like Blytheville, Osceola, Wilson, Marion, and West Memphis. Think of flat black fields rimmed by a scribble of scrub oak, of some of the best farmland on earth, of a proud, largely poor, and often under-educated people struggling paycheck to paycheck. Much like their sharecropper ancestors, they work each day with meager prospects, from "can see to can't see" as the indifferent sun passes them by overhead. Think of bottomland lying so low, every road's a levee. Think of Lehi, by all means.

GHOSTS

I come by my belief in ghosts honestly. While growing up mostly in Helena-West Helena, I was beholden to the only three TV channels broadcast out of Memphis. During the '60s and early '70s, I watched *Fantastic Features*, as did most every other kid in the Mid-South. Each Saturday at 6:00 p.m. on channel 13, a ghoulish coachman decked out in a black cape and top hat drove his black, horse-drawn hearse slowly through the dismal mist and into our living rooms. He was Sivad (pronounced Suh-vaad), our "Monster of Ceremonies." Sporting vampire fangs, white gloves, and a thick southern drawl (think "Bubba" Stoker) Sivad indulged in bad puns, corny jokes, and ad nauseam alliteration to introduce B movies about ghosts, Martians, and that house on Haunted Hill. Early on, I soaked up only the scary, shuddering every time Sivad looked over his left shoulder before opening the hearse to unload that scuffed-up coffin. An over-the-top score of gothic orchestral music rose to a shriek, as Sivad reached down and lifted the coffin lid:

fog rolled out from the dark mouth, along with the words FANTASTIC FEATURES, dripping in blood.

What was creepy to me as a child grew campy with age. The stuff of nightmares gave way to corny playground impressions of Vincent Price and Bella Lugosi. Sinister Sivad, turns out, was actually mild-mannered Watson Davis, a church-going, kid-loving auto mechanic from just up the road in Clarendon. He'd concocted his stage moniker one day by writing his surname backwards (Davis = Sivad).

But things continued to go bump in the night in ways Schlock Theater never depicted. Our town's various industries threatened to close up shop and, literally, "go south" if workers didn't fall in line. The final throes of ingrained segregation raged as our public schools were integrated by court order and white flight began in earnest. Big Ag rendered obsolete many livelihoods and further depopulated the area. Our nation's draft board continued to draw small, numbered capsules from jars. Each one declared the odds that some young man fresh out of high school would be conscripted to wage war in Vietnam.

And then there was Rosie, my light, the black woman who spent her weekdays in our home as a housekeeper and nanny while both my parents worked. I still catch myself thinking of her as "our maid," while being equally emphatic that Rosie was family too. It's complicated. I'm white, male, an only son, hence implicated in more ways than I can count. I also attended high school at a private academy for white students only. When I later packed for college, a Confederate flag was thrown into the box with the black-light posters and eight-track tapes. Custom drapery for my dorm window. So maybe this explains why some afternoons, when Rosie had had her fill of it all, or maybe just of me, she'd sit down to spell her bones—then jar my complacency with straight talk about the atrocities of the Jim Crow Delta. There had been lynchings, she said. Had I ever heard of the Elaine Massacre of 1919? I hadn't. It had taken place just a few miles south of town. Though known across the nation as one of the worst race massacres in American history, it was too close to home to be taught in school. Our history books lacked a few chapters, including one about the Red Summer of 1919. Besides, we were too busy being drilled to duck under our desks as a surefire antidote to the Red Scare and the nuclear arms race. Even today, you won't find a single historical marker in or around Elaine commemorating those who died in the slaughter.

Fear was in the air all across the Mid-South. Whether by fluke or some eerie coincidence, many towns held their weekly civil defense tests at the exact time *Fantastic Features* was being aired. In one ominous broadcast, the creepy notes of the opening title sequence fused with the high alert shrill of the air-raid siren. Knock-off Shostakovich swelled into a singularly menacing blare. Our scary monsters trumped Sivad.

GRACE

I'm still haunted these many years later, but more by love and loss than ghouls. I've come to take heart in Wendell Berry's poem "Manifesto: The Mad Farmer Liberation Front." Each day I seek to "be joyful though (I've) considered all the facts," to "do something that won't compute," to "practice resurrection." Fitful attempts at such grace over time have begun to displace my fear, and the sinister has slowly surrendered to the sacred. At my age, I'm foolish to take anything for granted. Today, tomorrow—even yesterday can be up for grabs. When I return home to the Delta, around most every corner I'm struck by what is no longer there and can only be accessed by memory now—the old home place, Turk's Auto, Beech Crest Elementary, that sweet gum in the Boyce family's backyard whose branches held the safe, consoling sway of my first tree house—all gone, boarded up, or cut down. Each is a compelling occasion for *memento mori*, sure, but even more, I'm given a chance to see what persists in this world that is my own but not my own. I still "see" places with the eyes of my heart. When some brave soul tags along on one of my fool's errands back home, I cannot help but point out what once was, but is now nothing. I stop, back up, and repeat the refrain: "Over there used to be . . ."

Places and things show themselves—but so do people. It's both typographical and personal, inscribed in the very idiomatic use of "here" for emphatic inflection: "This here . . ." "Now, listen here . . ." The common sense of here that addresses, that re-members, reattaches place with seeing and listening. "Now, see here . . ." you're liable to hear. "Where are you from?" is connected to "Whereabouts, exactly?" is connected to "Well, then, maybe you know_____ . Can you *place* him?"

Places and faces conjure one another. The landscape triggers what poet Gerard Manley Hopkins calls "inscape," the opening up of my most intimate inner life, rife with those I've known and loved. These ditches that drain Dyess were first dynamited and dug by sharecroppers like my grandfather Coley Johnson. These fields around Whitton were planted and harvested by small farmers like my grandfather Bill Proffitt. This laundry flapping in color on the backyard line was cleaned and hung by wives like my grandmothers, Christine and Agnes, who also chopped and picked these crops that begin where the yard ends. Their children, like my parents, Betty and Willis, were the ones who left the farm they'd helped run to pursue a better life. Many ventured north, to the automotive factories of Detroit, Pontiac and Flint, others to the surrounding towns and cities, there to sweat out the sweltering heat and thick humidity with a new lease.

Charis: grace, gift, the genesis of gratitude. All these givens. At my truest I trust both gift and Giver as bedrock. Folk like these in a place like this, where the sun blossoms orange at dawn and sets apple red at dusk. As emanations of God's grace, they bear prevenience: They "come before" me and set the precedent. They were the first to gift their gritty way into my life, to lay their hands on me, to lard my imagination with their Bibles, music, and myriad stories, to shelter me from the storm. They tethered me to a particular time and place. They let me go when it came time to leave. That time has passed, as have many of the places and their people, but still they live on in bone and blood and the thin places of the heart. Here I learned all the first things for the first time; here I return to relearn first things, even as I lean more fully into last things. One part grief, two parts love.

CONCLUSION

Delta, ghosts, and grace—this high-octane trinity fuels these poems. They have taken me back, but surely beyond sentimentality and nostalgia; and they've taken me aback, leaving me shocked, refreshed, with a more integrated sense of belonging that previously only flitted and flashed about as disparate memories, elusive as minnows. Each time I return, I'm better able to press on.

Italo Calvino once said that "the more enlightened our houses are, the more their walls ooze ghosts." I may not know beans about enlightenment, but I'm convinced of being companioned. The sheetrock of my consciousness is porous, plays host to myriad ideas, energies, and intuitions, allows memories to surface, gather steam, and compel, and recollects and projects lessons learned and blessings bestowed. Along with Flannery O'Connor, I have found my upbringing in the South to be "if not Christ-centered, . . . most certainly Christ-haunted." Whether by way of haunting or centering, a loving, living, wounded Presence permeates all these visitations, healing my mortal estrangement. I can't help but still myself before such enormity—and listen up. I do this best through poetry.

FLAT BLACK FIELDS RIMMED BY A SCRIBBLE OF SCRUB OAK

Come with me
to where I've been
and gone, a ghost
who can't quit trying
to breathe again
the air he once knew.

Sun-spangled ditches
flare silver from flat black fields
rimmed by a scribble of scrub oak.
Crowley's Ridge runs
like a loamy spine, or a welt,
down through the bottomlands,
all of it ridden—
by poverty, violence, segregation, the past—
into the river of my own slight
passage through this place.

Come,
hear the hanging hum of snake doctors;
settle in on the porch
as the mourning dove calls;
watch dusk descend till way past when
and the mosquitoes start biting;
know where the Savior blood
haunts, pulses, . . . spills.

Together, chances are,
we'll find a time and a place
on the far side of pig's feet jars
and sweet potato pie,
where the Delta's been done
and overdone—but
not undone—where
we might yet swing low,
grab aholt, and say grace.   +++

A Rare Hill Outside Dyess, Arkansas

PART I

Slowly he lifted his hands in the darkness
and held them in mid-air, the fingers spread weakly open.
If he reached out with his hands,
and if his hands were electric wires,
and if his heart were a battery giving life and fire to those hands,
and if he reached out with his hands and touched other people,
reached out through these stone walls
and felt other hands connected with other hearts—if he did that,
would there be a reply, a shock?

–RICHARD WRIGHT, *NATIVE SON*

Black Oak Grocery: Black Oak, Arkansas

CHICKEN TRAIN

chicken train running all day . . .
chicken train take your chickens away
               –OZARK MOUNTAIN DAREDEVILS, "Chicken Train"

Helena, I cross your bridge
where you wait, but not a soul
welcomes my return
to feel again the sting of your loss.

You know best how I waver
and amble in your heat, slow up
in your streets, a stranger
peeking through cupped hands
into empty storefronts, foraging
the vacant lots for what's in the veins.

Here it's early morning, forty-some years ago.
I'm looking up to my cousin Dennis,
who's come in early to open
Uncle Jake's store and start the coffee,
when the whole place buckles
into glass, plaster and bricks. Nothing but
foundation and grass now, where the dust
settled to rubble, where I pause to study my shoes.

chicken train take your chickens away

This face reflected back
from the ticket booth
window of the Malco Cinema
on Cherry Street is not me,
there's not enough
hair, the face could smile
more, could slip
into sweat and song, funk
it up with mouthbow and harp,

chicken train
runnin' all day
chicken train
runnin' all day

to name what the naked eye can't see—
Momma's an Avon Lady all made up
to deliver Wild Country in collectible decanters,
Daddy's at Dominick's with Ernest
bent over a chili cheeseburger—
young and making it,
enough history
here to be haunted
by a mop hung out to dry
on a backyard clothesline.

laser beam in my dream
. . . like a sawed-off dream

Scatter-shot in the gut, trying
to name names and place faces—
nowhere to be found
the streetlight that spring night where
at thirteen I came *this* close
to kissing Belinda Crawford,
the Rex Motel Café where
I fed the pinball machine
my lunch money before school
while waiting on the bus.

can't get on
can't get off

Helena, who knew
the '70s would be your heyday?
Even then, you bored me inside
to Hai Karate cologne and *Kung Fu*,
air-conditioned, highball games of Risk.

chicken train take your chickens away

I had not yet
heard your song.

Not even the tangled sway
and squander of your kudzu
cascade could stop the erosion
of Crowley's Ridge, its locomotive
sprawl harangues the singular crease
you ride into the Mississippi, sets
me to supposing: these draped
trees and cliffs . . . a wedding
party, a feast of vows,
. . . or maybe pretty ponies?

can't get on
can't get off

Where your bluffs take me in,
here where there I go again,
into all that climbs, coils,
and ravages the untended.
Tendrils rise a foot a day
to baptize Confederate gravestones,
dogwoods, the red-rusted plow,
all borne home verdant
by spine greening out into the blues.

Helena, how far to come to here?
Back to flounce and peck
along your levee. The moon low
over the wide river
spells the one place
I know exactly where I am:
now walking deserted rails,
now on Cherry again, cradled
where dreams bud and beam
me back buck-buck-buckAWKing—

prodigal chicken
in your arms tonight.   +++

Cherry Street: Helena, Arkansas

Skyline from the Levee: Helena, Arkansas

KEEN LUCINDA

In response to Lucinda Williams' song "Where Is My Love?"

You must have just missed me, Lu.
That's all I can figure, given your knack
for lost love. So I get that we never met
in Helena, why you're sure as hell now off combing
Tupelo, Birmingham, and Gainesville, slumming
your second, third, and fourth choices
to no avail as the song trails off.

You're keen, Lu.
How'd you know to look first in Helena?
Fact of the matter, I was
most likely just off Cherry, stalking the river,
walking east along boarded-up York to where
that side-street ends and my levee begins.

That might explain why we missed each other.
I was not alright in myself.
My head was probably down,
scrambling another place and time
as now I creak up the levee
slow on these knees through Johnson grass,
and watch my step over rotting beams
and rusty rails—undone
by the way love smells
of creosote, how like a boy still
yoked I look both ways in crossing
the abandoned tracks and can't help
but wonder all along where
it all went, don't know where
it all goes,
know only how you and I are drawn
by our sweet lack
to the song of the unsung, where
the melody of must prevails,
where you keen, Lu, you
socket, you soul, you Helena.   +++

ON HEARING ABOUT UNCLE BILLY

In memory of William Wright

On one of those trips back home
to the Delta, a visit that always sighs
like it might be my last, the call comes
while walking across the sun-baked
parking lot of a Walmart
built way after I was long gone.

I wave on my daughter and friend,
then veer toward some quiet as Aunt Helen
duly notes many things into my ear
about that day, how the lawn chairs
were circled, how cousins were catching up
by telling forgotten stories, how she kept calling back
to the trailer in the orange grove
where Uncle Billy sat with a book:
Bill, you better get back out here!
You gotta hear this!
And how he could not.

She carries on long enough,
lulls me back to where I'm listening
only to a stray summer day spent stuck
to the black vinyl seat, perched before the dusty dash
of Uncle Billy's Hardy Lawn Service truck.
He's behind the wheel, and what he's up against
I can't see. From where I sit, a boy of ten,
he's making it all fine: both windows rolled down,
a Coke bottle sweats cold between my thighs,
Jimmie Rodgers yodels spooky wild
havoc from the eight-track player. The ends meet
all along the way: gears shift,
Uncle Billy sings along, the swelter moans
the sweetest current there is over lawns greener than green.
It's all distant trains; it's broke-down lonesome dark-blue
love; it's bustin' your butt for a buck—everything
Uncle Billy loves. I forget all about The Monkees.

It's my daughter now telling my friend
as they exit Walmart and scan the parking lot
that she knows exactly where I can be found:

Find the nearest vacant field.
He'll be out there by himself,
pacing back and forth like he knows
where he is, like he means it.   +++

Uncle Billy: Dyess, Arkansas

LEHI

My two sisters and I watch soybean fields fly
by in rows of green from the backseat.
The occasional tractor chugs distant and down,

coughs up dirt into the morning haze,
while sapped roadside houses, mostly vacant, sit
slope-backed beneath the slump of highline wires

as we drowse across summer's thick middle
on a narrow belt of two-lane blacktop
not even halfway to Grandma's.

How far to Lehi, Daddy?
Momma says, *Far enough.*

The road signs wavering in the heat
don't say, the map neither.
To know distance requires a name

known only by locals as what's left
of Lehi, where the blistered blue
highway picks up I-40:

this knot of two gas stations and a café
being the last call of commerce
before West Memphis.

This is about how the Bel Air comes to be
left idling with the air on, how we
have slipped back into the back

giddy with our Cokes and Tom's peanuts
and can't wait to leave now, how
Momma's alone up front, hurrying

Daddy with that look.
He's still outside, just off the curb,
sweating through one last drag.

Momma says, You're lettin' out the cool, Honey.

This is about how Daddy comes
to look over his shoulder
and stomp the gas

as we make our merge,
how Pegasus rears up red
over his head.   +++

Arkansas Delta

THIS BLANCHED ABRASION WE CALL *IN*

By now we grab our knees
after each basket. Our sweat
specks dark the grassless dirt
beneath us. We strain
for breath in a midsummer's sauna
where, at day's end, the game is hard
to figure; a frayed plywood backboard
with bent rim hangs, a shadow nailed
to a wooden post that leans
to catch what's left of the sun.

The sides have already been picked.
Shirts and skins alike ignore
their mothers' calls:
Let's finish this thing.

PJ cradles the ball at the top of the key, all elbows,
then drives, his dribble muted
by the dust we deem our court,
this blanched abrasion we call *In*.
We're all baptized, the Arkansas Delta's
straitened array of Baptists, Pentecostals, and Backsliders
way beyond tired with contesting fouls:
Just take it out. Our chests heave
for air we cannot hold as night tightens.

To block the hook and time the rebound
our ardor grinds the earth into fine enough
motes to become our very breath,
to be flung by the blue million
into next week, fine enough
to slip through venetian blinds or
be sucked up by the window AC
and spit out as a gray film
of unwelcomed whit and iota over
the coffee table and the family Bible.

Tomorrow we'll be back at school early
where hardly a one of us made the cut.
So determined, we turn on each other
for now as the basket's being swallowed
by dusk closing in from the woods
across the way, we're shades at our best
clamoring, pestled bits of hair, bone, and blood,
beset till one side wins by two
and we drop our guard: *Great game, man.*

We make our way back together, spent, ...
to TV, homework, and supper.
From all across the subdivision
the night air carries voices we know,
calls us home by our full names.   +++

Backyard Redemption: West Helena, Arkansas

SECONDHAND ALLIGATOR

In memory of Ernest Davis

The words hand-painted on plywood
by a wino named Booker T
swayed above Plaza Street and served
notice to all who entered my father's
used-furniture store, his first foray
into self-employment, in West Helena, AR:

PROFFITT'S TRADING POST
We buy, sale, or trade.

Weekday afternoons I'd walk in
beneath that sign from a day
at Woodruff Elementary
to find them in back near the Zenith
with Johnny Cash or the Cardinals:
most days the Judge, Wink, Ernest, and Shake
circled about my father's fat-cat connivings
to take what was left over for what it was worth.

Eminences, all: enthroned on broken-winged cherubim,
chipped keepsakes, sofas splinted good as new,
refugees from repoed homes or settled estates,
rendered *used* by a prior love or a heartache's kick,
too much drinking or not enough staying put, a giving-out
of the stove-in heart. Dented appliances, nicked and stained couches,
a fussy dresser drawer being tugged
by a girl with a baby on her hip in need
of a bar of Lifebouy and a little Pledge,
even some taxidermist's joke
of a stuffed alligator sporting a grass skirt and lei,
most every piece auctioned off up the river
at the mercy of another's first hand, passed
over, down, *yours today.*

I would have given anything
to be let in on the whole determined deal,
would have gotten a crew cut
to be folded fresh inside their used lot,
their radiant compliance to the coin
where I knew the stars above would
ripen red and delicious, *biteable*

and white
as a dream you cannot remember
hunkered against the sixties
well into the seventies—pot, vets back
lost and wearing the flag as britches,
that rare Burger Shack sighting
of a hippie or two passing through,
and boycotts being threatened
by the town's black majority,
afro'd, steeled,
crossing the line decked out in stacks—

all this swelling up slow and livid in the Delta
and resisted for dear life by the likes
of my father, well-cloaked behind quiet
gossip, razzing, and hushed bets over Cokes
about the new waitress down at the Win-Flo.

I was too new to have known
these men so versed in stout,
seething last things all gone now,
the town, too, mostly, along with
Mohawk Rubber and Chicago Mill,
gone maybe even knowing all along
that that stuffed alligator would outlast them,
be found one day scuffed up in my basement
minus the skirt and lei,
just the still-black eyes spotted
skimming the surface, waiting
wild in a cardboard box with *Goodwill*
scrawled on the side.   +++

Assembly of God: Dyess, Arkansas

Proceedings of the 15th Annual Session of the Rock Solid Association

Elder Daryl declares the 15th Annual Session
open, seated, and in working order.
The Rock Solid Association
of Old Time Baptists of Jesus Christ
sit solemn in pews before him,
reciting The Charter.
Deacon Holt knows Elder Daryl
by marriage and the Blood, knows, too,
the sting and welt of these words
held forth by heart.

Deacon Holt ain't been right in a month of Sundays,
not been a shining
light to sinners, not even a fit
father to his five children.
Cluster Belcher's on his ass at the mine.
Wife Rosalie by his side still can't
look him in the eye. Nothing feels blessed
on this pretty day as he shakes hands and sings some
songs of Zion, not nothing blessed
since that night he pressed the Devil's grip
'round her neck, though she knows now who's
head of the house, a house
that's about to go back
if the bank ain't apt
to cut a little slack.

Maybe if he walked the aisle again,
if he went up and dropped to his knees
at the altar and come clean,
just a man with a hope, his heart only
before Jesus, maybe then when he gets to the part
that says, "Our hope is to be a home
for all of God's children
who have been trampled underfoot"—
Jesus just might rise up
within again, he might could get back
to walking in brotherly love
'til the final trump sounds.
Maybe he'd quit seeing what was left
of that scared look on his Rose's face.

Elder Daryl reads the prayer list.
Brother Pervis raises his hand to say
his grandbaby's been born
without oxygen a little too long.
The doctors can't tell how things'll be,
but she's doing okay so far. Says we
ought to be shouting our lungs out
because we're so blessed.

It was then, the saints would later say,
that the Lord laid a hand on Deacon Holt.
Stood him straight up where he was.
Heard him whisper: *Pardon me, Pardon me . . .*
sideways out of the pew. Saw
him hasten slowly
like a man on far,
up the aisle to the altar,
his head down
deep, in pieces.   +++

MIDWAY

Once Mohawk Rubber closed shop
and Doughboy Plastics cut back,
the carnival bucketed into town,
a shaman's grin with neon teeth.
Fast-talking strangers played host
to our drubbed daddies
on the vacant lot by Turk's Auto and Salvage.
One carnie barks, *C'mon, step right up!*
Another, *Don't lean so far!*

You snarl, *That's only cotton candy,*
just spun sugar and food coloring.
Expect me to blush. But life was hard
to beat that late-summer night
when I burned to lag in line
and watch this girl about my age
hold a cigarette out from her hip
and stir the empty heat into a hive
of pink with a paper wand and
a sole smile.

On a plane from Dallas to Memphis
you might close your laptop in time
to look down on our clutched bouquet,
petals reeling wayward color against the black.
That's the magic,
a million imaginings rising from a tad
of immanence swaddled by the whole
spin and scent of the minstrel night.
You can't hear it, but that Tilt-A-Whirl
there, it's playing Deep Purple,
crushing "Smoke on the Water"
into what's small and passing,
pleasing—one more
immensity measured
against the want of the land.   +++

Momma John's Kitchen: Dyess, Arkansas

WONDER BREAD

Now fool might be my middle name . . .
                    –REM, "Strange Currencies"

Waiting was for the birds
in the backseat on big
trips to Memphis to visit
the zoo, or Aunt Helen and Uncle Billy.
So my sisters and I picked at each other,
or held our breath and counted
One Mississippi, two Mississippi . . .

over the bridge at West Memphis,
looking for a sign.

Wonder Bread in neon.

Each time, I swear, it shone,
lit against the sky
as we crossed the river,

kept me on
track: a billboard
bread truck with a bumbling
driver who always waved.
Innocent
of having left the back door
wide open, swinging,
flinging staccato sweet
loaves into the street
where a hungry dog gives happy
chase, catches bread like manna
in mid-air from a *Wonder* truck.

This sign
no one much remembers.
Even my sisters are fuzzy
some fifty years later.
I've asked around, but no one can place
what brought me such joy—
and sure distress—
for the *Wonder* kept moving,
sometimes on my left, other times on my right.
Would not stay put.
It was my first known
instance of not knowing,
of flubbing what others seemed
prone to in their sleep.
How certain they were
of whether they were
coming or going.   +++

Mr. Jones of Jones BBQ: Marianna, Arkansas
Winner of the James Beard Award

BIVOUAC

The past is never dead. It's not even past.
        –WILLIAM FAULKNER

Words came as they came,
like this one, an army word,
maybe by way of our Scoutmaster,
who, most days most of the day,
drove the Guy's Potato Chips truck;
but most likely barked into us
by the besieged sergeant in an army movie
that came as a bargain for a quarter
and a Safeway coupon, an early-bird matinee
compliments of a place and time:
Saturday afternoons at the Malco
in downtown Helena on Cherry during the sixties.

Bivouac—just the sound should
have made us goofy, like most
things did back then,
like one more Don Martin cartoon
in *Mad Magazine*
where sound turned tactile,
like hands
folding a paper airplane that suddenly find
their very phalanges plaited and tucked
by the sheer desire of reach and hold into flight,
palm-plump wings fumbling in thin air,
dragging the body as payload before crashing:
FAGROON KLUBBLE KLUBBLE! No, wait—
that's the sound of a collapsing building—but like that.
Or BLIT! That's the sound of an eye being vacuumed. BLOIT!
Hear that? That's Popeye's muscle popping up.
But *bivouac* was never our BLIT or BLOIT, never
the butt of any joke. We said it next to never,
just took it as gospel from the sergeant.

Words flurried between us once we were dropped off
and had ducked in under the marquee to put the slip
on summer's thick bore, out of our parents' hair,
eager and down into the air-conditioned dark
to feast on vintage war, the kind fox-holed in
European fields that nailed surefire glory
a far cry from the jungle rot dealt nightly
by the news over supper that made Momma turn the channel.

We ate our death well done
with the same clean, commemorative conviction
that pressed copper into the stolid Doughboy
statue on the north end of Cherry, our WWI sentry
caught mid-stride in time across from the courthouse
with a grenade clutched in his raised right hand,
a bayoneted Springfield in his left.
Crowley's Ridge rose over his shoulder,
where ghosts were known to crouch gray
behind the Confederate Cemetery's akimbo
gravestones and granite angels.
There we all hoped one day to park
and get lucky under the stars.

When the house lights dimmed
another word came
as the town's black majority,
squeezed for now into the balcony only,
began to get their fill and pelt us with their own
hisses and hoots and flicked flecks of crushed ice.
We threw back the one word handy,
the one we'd somehow vowed to grow into
before we knew what for, before
it became the unspeakable.

For now, we aped our elders' ire,
tried it on under our breath in swapped jokes,
chased it down scratchy with our Cokes,
hurled it into that dark place
over our heads and just a little behind.
We spit it out until we saw red,

just like our helmeted heroes before us:
Filthy Japs ... lousy Krauts.

But not *bivouac.* Never ever
said it, just took it in as air,
a sergeant's order as our day drained off,
leaving us surrounded and exposed.   +++

Malco: Helena, Arkansas

REX CAFÉ AND MOTEL

The pinball machine and jukebox
by the front door were allowed for minors,
while those of age did their own thing,
good and tired bones in booths
over coffee and eggs before the shift
at Chicago Mill, Mohawk, Doughboy,
where they'd punch the clock to make it:
above-ground pools, tires, veneer. Whatever
pays. Back they'd come, the regulars,
over burgers at lunch, over
All You Can Eat Shrimp and Frog Legs
on weekends, back
spiffed up on their own time.

Some knew better than others
the café was a front, a narthex
to the sanctuary, where
the faithful declared their worth
in rooms rented by the hour:
There's always a vacancy
at the Rex for sex.
For grownups who'd earned the right
to do Lord knows what with whom.
In the end, the food
might've rivaled the room key.

This is not about the grownups,
but about that brief time when the narthex
fit just right my pivoting appetite.
When I did what I had to do
to get my hands on all that
ruckus between the flippers
as the juke box played.
Pinball promises for the change
I redeemed out from under
couch cushions, or earned by
scouring littered roadside ditches
hours on end for empty Coke bottles
I'd bring to Big Star for deposits. Anything
for a little pinball change—
even my lunch money.

The Rex came calling early, personally,
on a school day while waiting for the bus.
All the boys told all the girls to watch
for Bus 8, then we dodged Highway 49
and ducked into the Rex.

My money, my game.
The machine eats the nickel
and comes to. I stab the plunger
with the heel of my palm,
eager for the ball's arc to feed us
motion in this moment, the cusp.
PJ has already pressed D6 three times
for his quarter, so The Beatles'
"Get Back" chimes in as the points
rack up. The flippers swat, frantic
bounce and ricochet score, the whole
laden world bucks iridescent in the a.m.,
the Special's now lit, blazing red by the second ball.
Credits bang out their forced applause.

Jojo was a man who thought he was a loner
But he knew it wouldn't last

"Get back, Jojo!" My buddies yell.
I'm Jojo, nearly nine minutes of
firestarter and flame. This machine's *mine*.
I taunt and goad, the Extra Ball's lit gold,
the solenoids crackle, blasting
bumpers so taut the ball pops the glass
all get out. Two waitresses now keep
their eyes on us. It's all red-lining, *this* close
to throwing a rod, to tilting the whole
garish shebang, and I'm in that sweet
right-through-me adrenal hum
that smells electric and courses capillaries,
that sweet insistent fit, fever, and flash
where God comes easy and all
the targets are down. For now
the snake's fangs are still rubber,
the dark's becoming
a dare.   +++

Birdsong, Arkansas

OUT HERE

The longest nights are when after
another sales meeting in Memphis
my daddy comes home way late
for supper with the miles in his eyes
and they're at it again.
So instead of going to my room
I've taken to sitting
on these back steps. Out here
I can walk
over to the rutted side yard
and press my hand on the hood of Daddy's
Satellite still hot to the touch. Out here
I can hear
the empty Plymouth ticking
unsuring itself as the exhaust manifold cools
in the dark where he must now park
because this carport the realtor called
a double is lucky just to hold
Momma's station wagon
without scratching it. Out here
I can't help
buffered only by the back door
but take in the swell of havoc
within and wonder who's liable
to latch *what if* onto *where to*
to have my ear cocked to
the fading sound of a distant
semi as it pitches west and away
gear by gear gone on I-49
gnawing up the night.   +++

BONANZA

We swell with the move up:
a three-bedroom rancher, part-brick,
double-carport, new sub-division.
Black wrought-iron posts grace the front porch
and make life without a ladder a cinch.
With the TV on the fritz
and *Bonanza* on the way
my sisters and I are all eyes
as our fed-up daddy
climbs the ornate rungs.
He elbows up his belly
and shimmies over the gutters,
his brown Sansabelts and wingtips squirming
out of sight and onto the roof at last.

We run back inside to the living room,
tracking the creak of his steps overhead
as he lumbers up pitched shingles
into the July dusk to pause
before a startled metallic tree
whose thin, spinous branches jab
the indigo night for some nearer-than-now
promise, that something else we crave
cast from pray-tell-where
by way of WMC-TV in Memphis.

How's that?
Our Daddy's call is so faint, we still and listen hard
as he grabs hold and twists the antenna's trunk
or bends with care its razor-thin branches.
Any better?
We yell out our directions, scouring
the walnut-consoled blizzard
for any semblance of our heroes
leaping lucid on horseback through the storm:
No, wait, go back! You had it!

We are becoming literate in frequencies,
fluent tuners of the speckled
static into living color.
We are learning demand.
That's it! There—

He hears our silence as success
and lets go.
Careful not to bump or touch a thing,
he lowers himself to a firmer place, straddling
the roofline of his own sweet apostrophe.
He lights up a Kent. Through a plume
he looks out across West Acres
and catches the last of the streetlights
flickering on across his new neighborhood.

He checks his watch.
Sunday's almost gone.
Somewhere below a map's on fire. The eager
flames lick
through the Ponderosa and curl out.   +++

Willis Proffitt on Alice Street: West Helena, Arkansas

Chicken Graffiti: Clarksdale, Mississippi, Helena's Sister City of the Mississippi Delta

HAMARTIA

Turns out, the 3 a.m. racket in the coop out back
is a rout that leaves my rooster a red splat
in the feather-matted mud, spraddled and tossed
like a broken umbrella on this soppy night by a possum,

that timid filcher the Algonquin first named *aposoum*: "white beast."
That's close enough, so I stand in the rain at rake's length
in boxers, jab, jabbing like I mean it the soggy soft of his belly
until he hisses alive and scuttles out

the same sorry hole he'd come. Morning after, I'm back,
resolved by virtue of a sale on Havahart traps at OK Hatchery,
and a quick trip to the meat market, where they know
just the thing and slip me a lump wrapped in butcher paper

with an abettor's *No charge*. I read the trap's easy-set instructions
while all nine hens eye the shiny contrivance. They gawk and cluck,
a wary ruckus of small heads ticking nearer. Until I unwrap the bait.
Then nothing. The hum of flies. We fester in morning heat

over the butcher's call: the ordained chicken neck,
this pale, elegant peril between head and heart.
Too late now, I cinch the serous gullet
to the trap's trigger. The startled hens

still, then bob and scratch out
their own exodus, baw-w-w-king bit by bit away
from what these hands have gone and done,
leaving me to weigh what enemy I'd catch next.   +++

Helena Bound

Tell me where you're going, and I'll tell you where you're bound.
    —Jeffrey Foucault, "Train to Jackson"

Southbound Highway 1 to Helena,
the black Arkansas Delta fans out flat.
Dusk reaches from wooded edges
to shadow thin rows of green taken
still by what late fire the day holds.

I have been down this way before, small
eyes playing stern with the cambered
two-lane before me, all the while having slipped
the blacktop, waylaid by what the heart keeps at—
the levee beyond Crowley's Ridge to the east
so far holds fast the fitful Mississippi's crest,
crooked-line haze in the west, red-ball sun wavering low,
power-lines draping the roadside, stitched cross by haggard cross,
the train-vacant tracks.
Medieval reckoning says 22,560
atoms inhabit this hour.*

A banana-yellow crop duster
dips low and tags the last
of April's welter—jonquils, daffodils,
tulips and forsythia jut and whorl
from the ditchbanks and fencelines of
small white houses with scant yards
specked by dandelions—then banks
off, a spewed mist in the dot's parting.
Amber laves the land and hovers,
daredevil's last magic
before calling it a day.

By evening I'd hoped to have learned
even a little about all this carrying on, what lives
here that can't be left or rooted out,
this ... this ... this ...
packs the chest tissue taut,
more press than can be slaked
by where I'm going but can't get,
my raising that leaves me still
taken decades later, knowing
that plywood sheet
nailed across the storefront window
on Cherry Street is not the saddest thing
I ever saw, but for the 1000th time
I forget what is.   +++

Southbound on Highway 49 into Helena-West Helena

* Cf. C. Du Cange, *Glossariam mediae et infimae Latinitatis,* tom 1, p. 462

PART II

And they came to the Great River and crossed it, hoping
that by the grace of God no worse could befall them.
The place of the crossing is not known to exactness,
but certainly it was some leagues below where now
the town of Helena stands, in Arkansas:
Arkansas, from Akansa, U-gakh-pa, meaning
The Downstream People, or The Place of the Handsome Men.

–LILY PETER, *THE GREAT RIDING: THE STORY OF DE SOTO IN AMERICA*

Cafe Overlook: near Wilson, Arkansas

Momma John's Flowers: Dyess, Arkansas

CHICKENS IN THE RAIN

Run like us when they first hear
the sudden increase of leaves pattering
overhead, the gloved applause of trees
for these hens chickening out like we'd expect:
their rumpus retreat, their instinctive
forgoing of free-range living
for the dry and shiny confines
of the chain-linked coop.

My wife and I—quick, look alive—scram
like the kids we once were, once had.
Like cartoon villains we duck
soaked inside the Rubbermaid garden shed.
Beneath the rain rapping on the roof,
beside the mower, the leaning rakes and busted
bags of grass seed, breathing in the hint
of spilt gasoline and oil, comfort fills the space,
rills dull and soothing down the sides.
Our feathers are wet, but we're dry enough now
to watch trees, the pelted sway of the hammock,
what happens next to chickens in the morning rain.

How soon enough
they're back, peeking
eye by eye from the cooped dark.
One hen gives what's falling outside
her full what for: seven long seconds
of chicken contemplation—
then steps out and pecks forth,
clucking her resolve
through the downpour
for a swig of water,
her slick chestnut head
thrown throat back,
comb and wattle all, in
a full-body swallow.

That's when you
make a run for it,
knowing right then
that I will be left there:
still, dry,
divining the sudden burst.   +++

To a Green Patch of Yard

Before Big Ag beat
the Delta like a rug
and flung field hands
like motes to light
elsewhere for a spell
before being beaten
into flight again,

you weathered
the beginning of the end,
as neighbors grew sparse
and gave up trying to squeeze out
a living. They left

in front of your own eyes:
the rubble of charred chimney bricks,
a perfectly good hub cap, a V-8 engine
hung by a chain
from the bicep of an oak,
a smattering of unmentionables
flap like revenants in the yard
over shards of plastic and glass,
half-immured marbles
pock the cracked
gumbo beneath the cottonwoods'
dry clatter.

Marbles? Yes.
Before and after the departing
there were marbles
with the names you knew:
Aggies, Shooters, and Bumblebees,
Cat's-, Tiger's-, even Bull's-eyes.

Because there were children—
like your own—
children who knew better,
who got out and on with their lives
someplace else to ante up for keepsies,
who bore your grandchildren,
they and their ample lot
ever returning to the homeplace
to be greeted like giddy Magi
who want only to be met

by you, and led back
by hand up the dirt driveway
to a green patch
of yard north of the house
past the silver-spangled propane tank
and your irredeemable John Deere
that sits off by itself

in the shade that shuffles beneath
the Catalpa with a hollow chest.   +++

Momma John's Jar of Marbles

Mojo

We were raised with our share
of pets, mostly dogs.
The Pattons up the street
scratched by,
raised white rabbits in hutches,
but for food, to butcher
while Mohawk was on strike.
I raised chickens.
Built a coop in the backyard
behind the basketball goal.
Said it was for the eggs
but the hens all had names.

Tight on cash and soft on freedom,
in our town, none of them lived long.

Our mutt Mojo somehow
got hit and had the hoodoo
to survive a half-dozen times.
Being small and all fur, he
would manage to wrest
his matted, bloody body back
home, to rehab with more stitches than brains.
Each close call charmed Mojo
into all our prayers—and all
the burgers Momma would fry up
for him with a dab of Worcestershire.

He knew how to roll over.
You could sink your fingers
into his thick, white coat.
Smooth back the curls to
trace the small partings,
the touch of the raised
scars under the fur.
Jagged pink lines across the belly and back
spoke of rough luck, of the magic
of near misses
that made Mojo my brother.   +++

SHARP RELIEF

You're never far from home
just off I-40 where OPEN 24 HOURS
hums neon-blue against the Huddle House window.
Through the O of HOURS, you watch
the Red Roof Inn parking lot reel
in 90-degree heat at 9:00 a.m. where
two cowboy boots stick out from under
a U-Haul, an orange-and-white frigate
listing in the black sea's flare.

A ghost orchid blooms pink-white
from the truck's side, stemmed by the question:
Where will U go next?
while a woman in her twenties hugs a baby
and looks down on a flat tire
and her man in the boots who
finagles the jack.

Their other little girl's maybe three
and plays in slim shade
on a median of green
off a ways beneath a tree.
She's done up in her
red-checkered dress.

The jack's shot someone's
said I told you so he's down
to his T-shirt now punching
the spare with no air while
the baby squalls dead
certainties to no kind
end under the sun.
They're nearing check-out
and not even close
to down the road
and the hint of a job.

Her red dress billows.
She holds a brown plastic pony
with both hands. She's looking away.

If her father wasn't under it, jammed
up trying to jack this damn truck,
he would see she's too near
the road and yell
her back to her momma.
Before hollering he might,
at any rate, see her standing
still and all, and even
for a long second wonder:
What catches her eye?
What strikes her to light
at a place apart from
things so insistent and broke?

But tender love taut like
that is seldom seen
except in a new tense,
like when two guys in a gray
Dodge Diesel Dually
circle back by her real slow.   +++

WHAT MOMMA JOHN CALLED TO SAY

In memory of Christine Johnson

Momma John, Early Days: Dyess, Arkansas

Back in the day of answering machines
my grandmother called and left a message:
I called and you did not answer.

So.
Knowing my place,
I called back.

She'd fallen,
she wanted
to tell me.

It was March in Dyess, AR.
She'd already put out
her tomatoes,

the ones she'd been nursing
along since February, uncurling
greenseedlingsrising

into Better Boys
and Sweet Millions,
Tiny Tims, Totems,

heirlooms back
in the pantry,
where she put up

blackberries, butterbeans,
stewed okra, varied preserves,
her secret hot chow-chow.

Shelved walls,
years of jars
she canned.

Said she'd put all her babies out
early. Then, wouldn't you know, caught
wind of a cold front moving in

so cut the bottoms
from the dozen or so plastic
milk jugs she'd kept,

put on her mud-caked boots by the back steps,
slogged in the light rain
and gray chill past the smokehouse

to the garden plot.
capped each,
plant-by-plant,

thought, *That's right
cute, little
hats.*

Worked the grab and suck
of the black gumbo mud
step-by-step

till she wobbled and fell
back like a turtle,
flat-out on her silly back.

Stared into the cold-wet
rain falling
in her face.

Said, *I don't b'lieve*
I'm gonna put out
another garden next year.

Just lay there
looking up,
stared

down the dark
swirl above, heard
the rain beat

the tin tub
she'd set last fall
over the mower's engine,

came to
herself
before figuring out

how to pull
old bones up
from the muck,

before the boot-by-boot
march back
to the house,

before stopping
shy of the back steps
to stomp off the mud,

said to anyone listening,
Naw, I will too . . .
I b'lieve I will.   +++

Momma John, Latter Days: Dyess, Arkansas

THE FRONT

In memory of Bill and Agnes Proffitt

Till the weather comes
Granny's rope rug
is the perfect wrestling ring
as Berry Jack and I tag team
Sputnik Monroe and Tojo Yamamoto
and do our best Fargo Strut
in front of the rabbit-eared
Zenith Stratosphere.
Thousands egg us on at the Mid-South Coliseum
while Grandpa sits on the couch
mum behind the *Commercial Appeal.*

But when the weather comes,
we know to unknot
and look up—
not at the wide-tied weatherman
jabbering and stabbing the air
like a nervous auctioneer—
but at the one behind us
coming to
above the sports page:
the silver crew-cut,
the tanned face—
we watch him watching
till he's only saying it once.

We bolt for the pickup,
jump in the truck bed, stand tall as we can
with both hands knuckled to the cab.
Grandpa tears out, rattling down gravel roads
through fields of soybeans and cotton,
our faces full-tilt into
the smart of spattering rain.
We slow only to rumble
across frail wooden bridges.

He leans over the wheel
while Granny tries to dial in the latest
as we race to Deacon's place.
Where he's waiting, waving
us on in with a flashlight
toward the storm cellar.

He lifts the hatch.
We duck to follow his beam down
the steep wooden stairs.
Watch our heads. Step by step,
we dodge and swipe at spider webs
and look for snakes, till a match
strikes and flares out of the corner.
A kerosene lantern gets lit
and hung, swings from a nail
overhead, heaves haints
across the dank cinderblock walls.
But no snakes.

The smell's alluvial, loamy,
and we find ourselves beset
by past harvests, sit hedged
by shelves of preserves, mason jars
of apple jelly, peach jam,
and stewed tomatoes.
We're close in, listening
knee-to-knee on wooden benches,
looking mostly up, hunkered
beneath the wrack and roar, the
clatter of the corrugated tin hatch,
its lightning-lit seams.

Till all at once
the quiet . . . in whose wake
we follow the grownups
in slow ascent,
spilling out of the earth
into the night air
as the front muffles
off to the east.   +++

Wooden Bridge: Whitton, Arkansas

Bad Memory

In honor of James Dent

Cousin Billy asks if I remember
blowing up toadfrogs.

Says think back fifty years
to when it rained toadfrogs,
everywhere frogs at dusk,
so many it busted us up
beneath the light pole
hopping about in the that small glow
before the great darkness
where the yard gave way to soybeans.

Remember how it took two
to hold their fat bodies,
pry open their mouths
with leftover Lady Fingers and Black Cats
that stuck out like small cigars?
We lit them and watched
frogs fly.
Says he'll never forget
that crazy-ass laugh of mine.

I never allow that I do,
not the laugh, not
the frog piss wet on my hands,
their soft bellies and dry warts,
my dark glee over what I held,
the weaselly look
over each matchflare in the night
to see if my parents
were home yet from work,
the wick sparking over their beating throats,
how I couldn't stop myself as the light
in my eyes went out—don't remember
how I couldn't sleep either:

unsure whether toadfrogs had souls
but sure as hell knowing the great darkness
was all mine.   +++

Lawn Art: Jonesboro, Arkansas

LATER

The summer our knack
for Kick the Can arcs to Spin the Bottle,
we rush supper to fling ourselves
into orbit with Angela and her sisters.
Delight declares itself in the rank Delta night,
draws us out after dark to that lit knoll
beneath the streetlight, where we vie
with the prior whir and winged havoc
of beetle, mosquito and moth.
We tease and pick the mown
grass, damp already with July's early dewfall.
It grabs hold at the ankles, clings
to bare feet, shinnies up tanned legs
and skirts under the fringe of cut-off blue jeans.

We pluck the green stems of Bermuda,
lift them slender to our lips
like our parents' forbidden cigarettes,
slip dandelion barrettes into the tropical smell
of long hair, shiny with *Sun In* and *Prell*.

It still takes a game.
By turns, the Coke bottle spins and stops.
Points. Permits our closing in
out of the light and back
behind the blue hydrangeas.

Later, we say to the girls, as we take off.
Later, to our longings so sated for now.
Later, to the play of our regal nights,
the braiding of clover into crowns,
careful for now always
to wear them blossom-side out.   +++

TELLING TIME

For Hannah

My only daughter says, *Remember*
that time you took me
to the center

of what's left
of Dyess, AR, Johnny Cash's hometown?
Remember that?

Then commences to tell
how, of all things, I pointed
to a vacant cinderblock building

that shone bright white
with recent paint,
like it had just landed from Planet Radiant.

How I said, "That's what remains
of Huff's Lion Station.
You'll have to imagine

the sign,
the single island
of pumps,

the snowy black-and-white TV
where I watched astronauts
take their first moon steps

across
the Sea of Tranquility
down onto the shoulders of my grandfather and his buddies

who sat on wooden Coke crates,
their backs bent over dominoes, suspicious
of a Hollywood fraud in the Arizona desert."

That
  was 1969.
You were 13 then.

You're my daring
keeper of time. *I remember*
where I was when I was 13 too.

But I was still in orbit,
spinning weightless four decades
distant. Thinking only

in a lunar miracle
on a sultry Monday afternoon
in July at Frank Huff's.

Know how I know I was 13?
That's how old I was when I heard
on the radio that Johnny Cask had died.

My small capsule splashes
back down in time, buoyant
in blue.

"I remember, Hannah...
your call, the first
that day, took me back."

Then and there, as now,
the press of quiet between us—
like that white-hot building

standing on the corner of
Planet Radiant
and Gone.   +++

Frank Huff's Station: Dyess, Arkansas

SECONDHAND SMOKE

In memory of Betty Proffitt

A white thread curls from the ashtray
and ravels into a knot over
you, a young mother not yet thirty
with two children and one more
on the way. I'm still at home.
Quaker Oats and Captain Kangaroo
are done so I'm in my pj's watching
you bend intent over the Singer,
sewing with your back to me.

I've no idea what thin pattern you cut,
what you're making or mending,
hemming in or letting out,
though I know the terms, have heard
your pitch, can say it: *Affordable.*
One day I will be the keeper of that word.

But for now I can only watch the penny
taped to the needle that spins
Nat King Cole's "Stardust"
from the veneered Zenith.
The sweet soothe of his voice,
made rich by too many Kools,
rises from the console to greet
ceiling-high the gathered smoke
and swirl across a ballroom floor.

Some discoveries come late in the day.
Not these. I am all eyes and ears,
even lungs. I take it all in
deep after you, this hazy fix
we're in, all except
for the weight I carry,
how like you I keep pressing
the dark groove, scratching
what's left of the black vinyl
for one more song.   +++

Doing My Best Father

For Willis Proffitt

Willis Proffitt Graduates from Wilson High School: Wilson, Arkansas

You say you can't travel
like you used to, but just yesterday
that was you behind the wheel
of the station wagon I'd managed
to pack without your or Momma's help,
a pure pressed-against-the-glass splat
making its way west to north on 49,
the two of us in what's left of the front
seat growing quieter still with every thin
town we drove through strung
from Helena to college in Jonesboro.
We never thought we needed an Atlas:
Walnut Corner, Poplar Grove,
Marvell, Brinkley . . . all along
fumbling for any reason to stop—
was it Wiener or Waldenburg
where we needed a shake?

It was only yesterday you circled campus
till we found Twin Towers, the men's dorm,
pulled in and parked the burnt-orange Volare, and sat
sizing up this world of necessities
moving in: students lugged bulging cardboard
boxes snaggled in plastic hangers, the world's
first disco ball floated by, teetering atop
a stack of towels erupting from a wicker hamper—

a strange mirrored-ball world as new to you as me.
You saw me take it in too, saw me
full-well struck, all wobbly, my right
knee doing the jimmy leg,
and said the one thing you knew
would get me out the door:
Son, just say the word
and we'll turn this ole buggy around
right now and go straight home.
That's me you see behind the wheel
now, doing my best father, quiet like you,
bound like Atlas to get up under it all
and shoulder the moment.

Once I'm gone, you'll be left.
Sure as the world, you'll choose
the quicker route home: Highway 1
through Harrisburg, Wynne,
Forrest City, Marianna, Walnut Corner . . .
across fields so low every road's a levee.   +++

Living Water

Sir, you have no bucket, and the well is deep.
—JOHN 4:II

Here you are, Momma, all mother
in black-and-white, and there in Kodacolor—
only snapshots now—
and in every other one there's that tiny white stem.
Here's one, a tad blurred,
my toddler eyes wide on you reaching in
to pull me from the backseat
of a '57 Pontiac Starchief Catalina,
two-toned, chromed-out with flared fenders.
Daddy has just said, "Over here, Betty."
So you squint up into the sun
and there, peeking out of your pocket, is a pack,
and stuck in your smile is one that's half-smoked,
because, of course, your hands are full.
You do what you can.

Your children came to count
on your consolation
after you laid us down to sleep,
how you would cough yourself up
for a glass of water in the middle of the night.
Kitchen light staves
golden beneath our bedroom door.
The sweet smell of Pall Malls.

When the call comes
about the spot on your lungs
we're grown and you're still young.
I grab aholt and heave
the news onto my back:
I saw this coming
and could do nothing.

The last visit home
you won't let us talk
about anything except
how you won't quit,
haven't had one in weeks,
have taken up walking again.
How the ad said
there's this doctor in Canada
who can help you beat the odds.
Every night your feet soak in his solution.
Jokes about your purple soles
and the new tattoo dotting your chest
are as close as we can get.

Until I ask about all the empty plastic
Borden's milk jugs rinsed and stashed
in the storage room off the carport.
You light up: *Oh, I've been fixin'*
to get to that. There's this healing spring
outside Farmerville folk swear by.
Somebody's gone and tapped it
so you can get all you want for free.
Wanna make a run?

More than anything.

I want to pitch these jugs
in the trunk of your black Cadillac,
drive you to Bernice,
stop at Bill's Dollar Store,
then head east on route 2
onto and through Farmerville
to a place beyond
the city limits that lives
only in the minds of locals.

I want to pull over
where the shoulder's worn wide,
where there's no room for anyone but us,
to step out of the air-conditioning
into the livid sun of mid-July,
the thick, bug-buzzed Louisiana heat.

There you'll point out the path.
I'll take your hand to rustle
slow down the ditchbank
into the savage growth
of tupelo, water oak, and sumac,
of wisteria gone wild and tangled
in my mind all the way back—

to Helena, honeysuckle, the Low Road
of twisted gravel to Storm Creek Lake
where you'd carry me as a boy
to scout out and gather cattails or mistletoe—

till a dark glade
now hits our faces Carrier cool
as the path gives way,
widens into a clearing.

Here the water spills silver
from a spigot, a small
shepherd's crook
beside a wooden bench.
Over our heads someone has tacked
a bible promise to a live-oak, something scrawled
about never thirsting again.

Here beneath the promise
you take a seat, huffing.
You sit and watch
while your only son
does what he can do.

Here he hands you his damp shirt.
He bends to top off, cap, lift
the first two gallons.
He turns away to lug them
back. His pale back
burns white up the dark
bank of violent green
till the roadside sun breaks
against the shade,
till on that shore you see him
catch fire.   +++

THE TIME OF THE SNOW

Late March is more winter than spring. Cold.
Rain falls and hail threatens all the windy way down
to El Dorado. I pull into your drive mid-morning and catch you
in the side yard studying a plastic waterfall, mid-assembly,
bought last week on sale at Home Depot
to force spring's hand. You look up
and drop the tangled heap of hoses and cords.

I never count on you saying much, don't
see it coming when over lunch you hold forth
how my birth found you some 57 years ago at 23
far from home a week before Christmas in Flint, MI,
on the assembly line at GM asking: *How much longer?*
How during the slow drive back from St. Joseph's
through the pewter slush to the attic apartment
off Saginaw, nerve stole new into you from the side
where your only son rode swaddled on your wife's lap.
You mustered the gumption to git, and lit out,
delivered us back among our Arkansas kin.

I come home hungry for Exodus,
take it in sweet with a bite, like barbeque. Know now why
the strange thought struck me on the drive down:
*If I had been born into the tribe of the Nez Perce
during the 19th century you would have told
Lewis and Clark that your son came into the world
at The Time of the Snow.*

Seeing you now at 80 as you see me
out to my Jeep, I know it's always been
all we could do to hold the line. We can't help
but dicker before goodbye: *Let's see . . .* we say.

The pitched waterfall, the white leaves
of unread directions pattering wind-pressed
against the chain-link fence. Our antics
shore up the base and check the connections
until the pump hums low and the spigot squawks
loose its own clean sheet of water
over molded stones from China.
Come fall, we'll revel in the raw
slip of silt and moss.   +++

Rivervale, Arkansas

Rivervale, Arkansas

In memory of Coley Johnson

is where morning catches hold.

We park and step out of the station wagon,
stretch, stand, and stare before unloading
our poles and bait, sizing up how the sun
splinters the morning mist and flecks
the Little River's turgid carrying-on
just three steps ahead.

From this bank you flare out over all
the world bygod as my grandfather
Coley Johnson before me. You point:
Yonder's a blue heron. And there is,
still and stick-legged on the far bank.
Of a sudden, it heaves off
as a red pickup pulls up easy to the river's edge,
dips down and deliberate into the brown
current without sinking or sliding and continues slow
across to idle solid astride the river's middle.
The driver's door opens. Out steps a shirtless man
in jeans. He's got a bucket and a sponge,
his black rubber boots sink barely ankle-deep
in the flow. He begins sudsing up the hood
as WMC AM 790 on your dial
wails Hank Williams into first light.

I'm at your elbow,
absorbed back-and-forth between
such things as this and you,
ancestral pulse,
as in a dream, as even now,
without wish or care
these things shine of themselves.

You grin and say: *I see, said the blind man.*

Look here now,
it ain't no Jesus miracle, son. Just a shoal.
Made that way way back when
I was no bigger'n you are now
and the Corps of Engineers
saw fit to tunnel the Right Hand Chute
of the Buffalo River drekly under
this here Little River.

Rivervale, I learn, as we bait our hooks,
is new only to me; it precedes even you, was once
shaken like a great rug by the New Madrid earthquake and left
a swamped and tilted thing, a slough
the Corps sought to channel, to render arable,
so dredged and drained tame.

You cain't see it, but
there's a concrete slab running
yonder under that truck.
Tops out the culvert they laid.
When it's dry like now
and the Little gets low,
the current's weak enough
to drive out on it, like where this here feller's at,
gittin' a free car wash.
Course now, you gotta watch yourself,
folks's slipped and drowned here too.

I squint through the mounting morning heat
to the red shimmer, then back to you, all in
with the whir of myriad heed:
blue heron, river sheen, red pickup, the prospect of
hidden flow underfoot—and of slipping.
Fact of the matter
there's what's happened
and them what's happened to.

Then we drop our lines.   +++

GASOLINE

If you wanna get to heaven,
you gotta raise a little hell.
　　　　　–OZARK MOUNTAIN DAREDEVILS, "If You Want to Get to Heaven"

Blame's got little to do
with how he proves his mettle
tonight in the back parking lot
of the Holiday Inn. It's not the pot,
his exhausted parents, the sagging small
town on the brink. Stark prospects alone
can't set him on such a tear, can't
say what praise and praise alone knows:
his obeisance stoked by the jumpy gods
to seethe by day and drag the night.
In stacks and frayed bell-bottomed denim
he ducks behind the rear
bumper of a '73 Cadillac Coupe Deville:
chrome rocker molding; Soft Ray
tinted glass—the same late model and make
his father swore just last week
he'd one day own.

In the moonlight a green garden
hose stems out and over the Caddy's Ohio plates.
Down to his knees, he sucks
hard in the hope this time
he won't swallow—and prays,
lit lanky in the blessed heat of *mine* and *take*,
prays *it'll all be better,* prays *pray for me*:
praise, praise his sky-blue bug on full,
praise the lucent June night,
praise Cherry Street stoplight by stoplight,
praise stolen looks at girls
he'd never dare ask out,
praise Big Star in his ear,
high test in his throat, the scent
of gasoline everywhere
dripping stout from his hands.　　+++

Sweeney Motors: Harrisburg, Arkansas

An Early Exit

My eyes grow weary with gazing upward.
            —Isaiah 38:14

I

"We don't get out much anymore."
That's how she puts it, trying
to swat a fly and finish telling

her pastor why her Coley
keeps holed up in his shop
out back with this hankering

to put life in a headlock
and squeeze until there's a pop
and blood from the nose,

why there's no more church,
not with those Holy Rollers
leapfrogging in tongues to impress.

God? Sure, but even so.
"His knees ain't what
they used to be."

I nod. Either way,
amen. I stand
too soon to leave.

She knows, so says,
"Don't take it personal, Preacher.
He's always been determined.

He just sits out there and sharpens
saw blades all day. I swear, he's done
rolled up his life with his sleeves."

The dry breeze carries her words from the porch
over my shoulder toward the arid, alligatored fields,
green stalks low for July, their level best

given the little rain we've had.
She can't stand to see Coley's rawboned head
spend itself bent

over a wheel of sparks
spraying into nothing.
The edge he sets

I can see. Safe in my car,
backing out, I manage
a smile as she waves.

II

Time was, a church potluck
one early May saw Coley hunkered
obeisant with the rest of the men

on his heels beneath the big elm.
He sized up the bottomland on all sides, the dark
gumbo muck, furrowed and flat and lying in wait,

till a grin cracked loose from his head:
"Like they say, 'You stick with it all summer,
and it'll stick to you come winter.'"

We laughed as he rose, not knowing
where the Spirit goes, that he was about
done, and sure to get shed of us.   +++

Coley Johnson's Shed: Dyess, Arkansas

ACKNOWLEDGMENTS

Well... how did I get here?
        –TALKING HEADS, "Once in a Lifetime"

This book was made possible by the gracious attention of friends, family, and teachers, particularly: Scott Darwin and John Harrison, two of The Three Amigos who accompanied me on a thousand forays through the Delta; Belden Lane, my *anam cara*, Soul Friend, whose gentle yet persistent push gave me the courage to give this book a go; Matthew Lippman, enthusiastic genius of a poet, mentor and editor; Hannah Minchow-Proffitt, my daughter and gifted graphic designer; Elim Allee, my son-in-law and first-rate photo editor; Rebecca Starks, generous friend, poet and editor-in-chief at *Mud Season Review*; Christina Taylor, devoted publisher at Middle Island Press; Rev. Johnny Burns, my faithful companion and fellow pilgrim to the annual King Biscuit Blues Festival; and Steve Hollaway, Chuck Hussung, Coles and Leslie L'Hommedieu, Drew Phillips, Daye Phillippo, Guy Sayles, Douglass Sullivan-Gonzalez, and Wendy Vogenitz-Tinsley, my patient allies, for their close attention and encouraging input.

You have all borne the brunt of my deep resonance with the saying, often attributed to mystic Meister Eckhart: "Only the hand that erases can write the true thing." I'm drawn to the necessity of *erasing*. Poetry has taught me to erase my way to what's new and true and alive. Revision is writing. I hold forth, then pare back. I am at my best when I trust this give-and-take process, when I properly regard words as having a life and intent of their own. As George Saunders says, "Revision is an act of love in progress." So I try to be, as he encourages, "hopeful and generous, but not too pushy." For me, this requires a patience I don't always have, so I need a community of readers. Thank you for being there, for looking over my shoulder in love.

I'm grateful to the Ozark Mountain Daredevils for their generous permission to include the lyrics of their song "Chicken Train" in the title poem, and, further, for allowing me to use the same title for this book. John and Steve, your praise and encouragement have carried me through, like the arms of brothers. Such encouragement and support are pure grace. I've been a fan of the Ozark Mountain Daredevils for years. For more about that, email me at thechickentrain@gmail.com. For more about the amazing Daredevils themselves, go to: www.ozarkdaredevils.com.

About the Contributors

Poet

Terry Minchow-Proffitt is a pastor and poet living in St. Louis, Missouri. These poems stem from the eastern Arkansas Delta of his upbringing. Given half a chance, he's liable to hold forth about Johnny Cash as his favorite contemporary mystic. Terry's poems have appeared in numerous journals and magazines. His chapbook, Seven Last Words, was published by Middle Island Press in 2015.

Many of his published poems, essays, and occasional musings may be found at www.terryminchow-proffitt.com.

Designer

Hannah Proffitt-Allee is a graphic designer and lettering artist based out of Portland, Oregon. When she isn't designing her dad's books of poetry, she's busy exploring the Pacific Northwest's beautiful landscapes. Hannah is always looking for new clients to collaborate with to make something meaningful together. If you are interested, contact her through her Etsy shop: Batch Lettering Studio.

Publisher

Christina Anne Taylor is the publisher at Middle Island Press and a poet (*Villanelle & Varia,* 2010) living in West Virginia. Through Middle Island Press, Christina helps authors from all over the country make their publishing dreams come true.

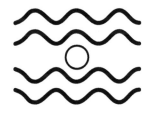

2016   Middle Island Press

Made in the USA
Lexington, KY
17 January 2017